DOROTHY HOLE

THE AIR FORCE AND YOU

CRESTWOOD HOUSE
NEW YORK
MAXWELL MACMILLAN CANADA
TORONTO
MAXWELL MACMILLAN INTERNATIONAL
NEW YORK • OXFORD • SINGAPORE • SYDNEY

ACKNOWLEDGMENTS

Special thanks to Steven M. Hughes, Staff Sergeant, United States Air Force and Robert J. Gonzales, Jr., Captain, Public Affairs Office, United States Air Force

PHOTO CREDITS: *All photos courtesy of the United States Air Force.*

DEDICATION

For my son, James Macpherson Hole

Cover design, text design and production: William E. Frost Associates Ltd.

Library of Congress Cataloging-in-Publication Data

Hole, Dorothy.
    The air force and you / by Dorothy Hole. —1st ed.
    p. cm. — (The armed forces)
    Summary: Discusses life in the United States Air Force, how to join this branch of the armed forces, and how to prepare for a future career while still serving.
    ISBN 0-89686-764-1
    1. United States. Air Force — Vocational guidance — Juvenile literature. [1. United States. Air Force — Vocational guidance. 2. Vocational guidance.] I. Title. II. Series: Hole, Dorothy. Armed forces.
UG633.H56 1993
358.4'0023'73 — dc20
            92-9774

CRESTWOOD HOUSE
MACMILLAN PUBLISHING COMPANY
866 Third Avenue
New York, NY 10022

MAXWELL MACMILLAN CANADA, INC.
1200 Eglinton Avenue East
Suite 200
Don Mills, Ontario M3C 3N1

Macmillan Publishing Company is part of the Maxwell Communication Group of Companies
First Edition
Printed in the United States of America

10   9   8   7   6   5   4   3   2   1

CONTENTS

This is a view of the Randolph Air Force Base in Texas, as seen from a U.S. Air Force helicopter.

CHAPTER ONE

HOW DID IT HAPPEN?

The noise of the helicopter roars in your ears. From a few hundred feet in the air, you look down on a desert that reminds you of cowboys, cattle rustlers and wagon trains, but you're halfway around the world from the American Southwest. That dry, forbidding land belongs to Turkey. You are on a mission of hope, bringing food, medical aid and friendship to a desperate people, the Kurds.

You are part of Operation Provide Comfort of the Special Operations of the United States Air Force. Hundreds of hungry men, women and children, with arms outstretched, rush to surround you as you step from the chopper. When you joined the air force, you never dreamed you'd be involved in a mission like this.

It all began the day you walked into a **recruiter's** office. The recruiting sergeant shook your hand, pointed to a chair beside the desk and was ready to answer your questions. You had so many you wondered where to start. The most important was, "Should I join the air force?"

Only you can decide. No one can give you the answer. The recruiter can tell you the facts about length of enlistment, benefits, pay, housing, training, skills to be learned, your chances of flying and much more. But you *and you alone* must debate the reasons why joining the air force is right—or not right—for you.

Air force life differs from that of a civilian. Before you enlist, think it over carefully. Ask yourself, "How well do I know myself? How will I react to danger? Can I be happy living in a foreign country? Do I get along with people, and am I friendly? How good am I at taking orders?"

The last question may be the most important. As an **airman**, one of the first things you have to learn is not to question an order. Incidentally, if you're a woman, you have to get used to being called an airman. That term includes both men and women.

Do you hate the heat and wilt when the temperature is over 100 degrees? You might be stationed in Saudi Arabia. Do you suffer in the cold? Are you scarcely able to breathe when the freezing air hits your lungs? The air force has **bases** in Alaska too. You have to go where you're assigned, no matter what you think of the place.

If you don't like the people you work with, it's too bad, but there isn't anything you can do about it—except wait to be reassigned or for your enlistment to be up.

(Photo right) This F-117 bomber is used by the air force in military operations. As a member of the air force, you will have the chance to learn about machinery like this.

Some people feel trapped living on a base. You may not like being surrounded by the same people at work, at play and as neighbors.

It's possible you may feel as though you've lost control of your life.

Others love being airmen. You may be one who enjoys living in a protected area. You feel safe. Crime doesn't worry you. Maybe you find you like it so much you don't want to live anywhere else.

In peacetime you are not exposed to any more danger than you would be as a civilian doing the same job. In wartime the amount of danger you experience depends on your job and where you're stationed. Your **unit** could be sent to a base near the fighting or to a place that is a **bomber** target for the enemy.

You listen to the recruiter list the many benefits: full medical and dental care; 30-days of leave with pay each year; the many jobs for you to choose from that are needed to keep the planes flying; a steady paycheck; a chance to live away from home, to see the world, to learn a new job skill to take back with you to civilian life if you decide the air force is not for you after all.

When the recruiter pauses for breath, you ask, "Will I get a chance to fly?"

There are many skills for an enlisted airman that require flying, although you must be an **officer** to be a pilot or a navigator. You go up in a plane if you decide—and if you qualify—to become an **aircraft loadmaster**, a "boom" operator on a **refueling plane** or flight engineer, among other jobs.

A lot will happen to you before that day arrives.

CHAPTER TWO

GETTING READY

You're thinking about joining the air force. You want to talk it over with someone. You know you must register at the post office when you're 18, but what's involved when you sign up for the air force?

Discussing it with your school counselor or adviser is a good idea. By speaking to your teachers and reading your school records, your counselor probably knows more about you than you realize. One of the first things your counselor will advise is that you take the **Armed Services Vocational Aptitude Battery (ASVAB).**

To get into any of the armed services, you must take this test. It is one way of learning more about yourself. It can be helpful to you in preparing for the future, even if you don't join the air force.

From this test the air force will learn what type of job skills you already have or are able to learn. You may have talents you

The Armed Services Vocational Aptitude Battery is designed to help the air force learn about you and also to help you learn more about yourself.

don't know you have. The air force wants to be sure you will be assigned to a job you are capable of doing and that you will enjoy.

A large number of subjects are covered in the ASVAB; among them are mechanics, arithmetic, problem-solving skills, general science and word meaning. The air force doesn't expect you to be good in all subjects. Your local library has books to help you study. Try taking the sample tests. If your answers are incorrect, figure out where you went wrong. This will help you when you take the real test.

See how well you do with this:

"An eclipse of the sun throws the shadow of the:

A. moon on the sun

B. moon on the earth

C. earth on the sun

D. earth on the moon"

Think carefully before answering.

Yes, you can flunk. Don't panic! Take it again after a 30-day wait. If you fail this second time, you have to wait six months before trying once more.

Some schools invite a recruiter to speak about the ASVAB so you and other students will understand the results of the tests. Find out as much as you can about your scores. You learn what subjects are your strong ones and what are your weak ones. Use this information in choosing what you want to do in the air force or in civilian life.

With the ASVAB behind you, now is a good time to visit the recruiter. Are you too young? If you are 17 years old (the youngest you can be to join), you need the consent of your parent or guardian. After your 28th birthday, you will be too old to join.

The air force accepts both men and women. The same requirements apply to both. Whatever is necessary for one is

true for the other. Women make up a larger percentage of the air force than they do of any of the other armed services.

If you were born in the United States, proof of citizenship is required. You must have your birth certificate and social security card. You don't want to lose these documents; bring them along only when you decide to enlist.

You must prove you are a citizen if you were born out of the country and your parents are Americans. If you were born out of the country and your parents are *not* Americans, you must show proof that you entered the United States legally for permanent residency (a green card).

The air force requires you to be a high school graduate (only 1 percent of recruits are not). This service is very education-minded. They hope you want to continue studying and offer a variety of ways to help you pay the costs. At the moment you may not be interested, but don't close your mind to it. Your recruiter can tell you about these programs. Read the brochures. Who knows what you'll think three years from now?

(Photo left) It's a good idea to ask the recruiter any questions you may have about the ASVAB or about the air force in general before you decide to enlist.

These recruits are receiving training in the field of mechanics. You may qualify to receive training in the field of your choice in the air force.

CHAPTER THREE

MAKING UP YOUR MIND

Now that you know the papers you need, you're anxious to learn exactly what you will be agreeing to if you do join the air force.

For instance, how many years will you be committing yourself to serve?

Enlistment can be for four or six years **active service**. You actually agree to serve for eight years. The remaining years are spent in the **inactive reserve**. During that time you have no air force duties. However, in time of war, you may be recalled to active duty. This happened to a great many people during the Persian Gulf conflict.

There are two main enlistment programs. If you qualify for the **Guaranteed Training Enlistment Program (GTEP)**, you can select from over 100 job specialties the type of work you want to do. *Always keep in mind that the air force must agree that you are capable of doing that job.* The air force gives you a written guarantee that you will receive training in that job skill and you will be assigned to a duty using that skill.

If you have completed three years of **Junior Reserve Officers Training Corps (JROTC)** in high school, you can enlist under the GTEP as an airman first class (an **E-3** pay grade). That means you skip the first two pay grades, **E-1 (airman basic)** and **E-2** (airman). There are other ways of doing this, such as winning an award from the Civil Air Patrol. Incidentally, although it is called JROTC, you do *not* receive an officer's commission when you finish high school.

The air force needs people in certain job specialties, and if you choose one of them, you receive a bonus. This is also true when you pick work that is considered dangerous. The jobs and the amount of the bonuses change with the needs of the air force. For instance, if you decide to become an **explosives ordnance disposal specialist**, you may receive a bonus of $1,000. Other skills receive even larger amounts. However, to be eligible, you must enlist for six years. Ask your recruiter for the latest information.

These bonuses are not handed out when you enlist. First you must successfully complete your training in that skill.

Suppose you've picked a job you would like to do and the air force agrees, but there is no opening; then what? You will be placed in the **Delayed Enlistment Program**, which assigns you to the inactive reserve. The duties of the active reserve are discussed later in the book. You remain a civilian in the active reserve until the air force has a place for you. It gives you a chance to complete any studies you may be taking. It can last as long as a year.

GTEP is one of two enlistment programs. The other is the **Aptitude Index Enlistment Program (AIEP)**. The AIEP is for you if you are interested in an air force career but don't know what type of work you would like to do.

The air force is divided into four areas to choose from: mechanical, administrative, general or electronics. You pick one of these four areas when enlisting. It is a general field, *not* a specific job. During **basic training** you decide the particular job skill you wish to do. Whether or not you'll be assigned to it depends on the needs of the air force as well as on your ASVAB, your experience and your education.

You've always wanted to be a fireman? Sign up for Fire Protection. You learn how to operate fire-fighting equipment,

Many of the skills you will learn in the air force can be of value to you even after you have completed your enlistment period.

help extinguish aircraft fires, be involved in rescues and practice first aid. If you don't reenlist, you have excellent training to become a civilian fireman.

Maybe the action in Aircrew Operations sounds exciting. You have frequent and regular flights. You might become an inflight refueling operator, a pararescue/recovery crewman or an aircraft loadmaster.

Riding in a plane with paratroopers during the invasion of Panama, one loadmaster's job was to open the door so the paratroopers could jump. Then he returned to his base, the only passenger on the plane!

Aircraft Operations trains you for one of many skills. Some of your job choices in civilian life include aircraft mechanic, cargo handler, electrician or shipping clerk, depending on the area in which you receive training and experience.

Until recently women could not be assigned to combat areas. The Congress of the United States has passed a law stating that women may now serve in combat operations, although they may not be involved directly in the fighting.

You still have some questions, such as, "Do I buy my own uniforms? Must I have a haircut? Where do I go for basic training?"

Under international law, you must be in uniform 72 hours after reporting for active duty. The air force supplies the clothes you need when you arrive at basic. After that, as an enlisted airman, you receive a clothing allowance to replace damaged or worn-out items. Uniforms must be kept in perfect condition.

Yes, if you're a man, your hair will be cut, probably shorter than you've ever worn it. If you're a woman, you're luckier! You can wear your hair any style you choose as long as it clears your collar.

And you may *not* have your car at basic training. Anyway, you'll be so tired at night, all you'll want to do is collapse on your bunk and sleep!

Where do you do basic? Where all **bluesuiters** do: Lackland Air Force Base (AFB), San Antonio, Texas.

When you're sure you want to join, the recruiter will ask you to fill in and sign an application form, just as you do when you apply for any job. This is *not* enlisting.

Most of the questions on the form concern your background, including where you were born and where both your parents were born. If you don't know some of the answers, take the form home. When you've filled in all the blanks, return it to the recruiter.

Signing the application does *not* commit you to enlisting. You can change your mind. It also does *not* mean that the air force is going to accept you. You might not qualify.

The air force is the first to admit that their service isn't for everyone. They want you to be *sure* before you take the oath.

Although you and your recruiter talked over the various skills, remember that a recruiter cannot promise you anything. This frequently causes misunderstanding. The guarantees are made at your next stop, the **MEPS**, or **Military Entrance Processing Station**.

CHAPTER FOUR

"I SOLEMNLY SWEAR..."

The day you report to the MEPS will be one of the most important days of your life. Decisions that affect your future will be made. When you leave the station, you will know if you meet all the standards—physical and mental—that a new air force **recruit** must have. And if you do, you sign a legal contract with the government, take the oath and return home an enlistee.

MEPSs are located in large cities throughout the United States. If there isn't one near you, the air force will pay for your transportation to the nearest center. As the day starts early—you must check into the MEPS between 5:30 and 6:30 A.M.—the government pays your bill at a hotel so you may spend the night before close-by. The next morning, after breakfast, a recruiter will drive you to the Processing Station. Be sure to bring all the documents the recruiter listed: driver's license, social security card, birth certificate, green card, high school records and whatever else is required.

(Photo left)   Be sure that you have considered all of the pros and cons before you take the air force oath!

Recruits from all the armed services are processed at the same stations. Usually your physical examination comes first. Don't forget, if you wear glasses, even if only for reading or driving, bring them along. The same goes for contact lenses. So much the better if you have the lens prescription; tuck it in with the other papers.

If you wear braces on your teeth, your dentist should give you a letter stating when you will be finished wearing them. You cannot enter active duty until your braces are removed.

You will be tested for alcohol and drug abuse and HIV, the virus that causes AIDS. Your height and weight will be taken. Tell the air force about any major surgery, illnesses or broken bones you've suffered through. If possible, bring copies of your physician's records of treatment you have received. The doctor examining you determines if you are physically fit for the air force.

Those who haven't taken the ASVAB must do so before going to the MEPS for their physical.

Before lunch you go to the **Entrance National Agency Checks (ENTNAC)**. You'll be fingerprinted and interviewed to discover if your enlisting in the air force is a security risk to the United States. Your fingerprints are sent to the FBI, where they become part of your military records.

By now you're hungry. If you eat in the MEPS dining room, your food is free. If you go outside the building, you have to pay for your own meal.

Now comes one of the most vital interviews of your life. If you are entering under the GTEP, you talk with an air force liaison or counselor. You know the work you want to do; the counselor knows what you're qualified to do. Sometimes these are not the same. Matching them is done with the help of a computer.

All enlistees are required to pass a physical exam before they can become part of the U.S. Air Force.

The computer already knows the expected vacancies in the air force. The results of your physical, the skills that interest you, your ASVAB scores and the date you can report for duty are entered. The computer displays openings in the skills in which you are interested and that you are qualified to do.

Almost every job in the air force is one that, if you decide not to reenlist, has a twin civilian job. Take **avionics systems**. It includes installing, maintaining and repairing automatic

Training is offered in many high-tech specialties of the air force. You may be able to apply this training to a challenging and rewarding career.

flight control systems and radio and navigational equipment. In civilian life that could lead to work on electronic aircraft systems on just about any type of aircraft at almost any airport.

Choosing mechanical/electrical skills might result in your being an electrician or heating and ventilation worker, among other jobs. And vehicle maintenance means you could fix your own car at no extra cost! The list of skills seems endless, including food service, personnel specialist, accounting, dental and many high-tech specialties, as well.

No matter how nice the recruiter is, no matter how helpful the interviewer is in trying to match your interests with job openings, *do not* sign the enlistment contract until you are completely satisfied. This is a legal contract that you must honor. The skill you pick as your first choice may not be available. You should be flexible enough to sign up for one or more areas of interest in case this happens.

The enlistment contract names the job you have requested only if you enter under the GTEP. This does not apply if you have entered under the AIEP. In that case your contract will show which one of the four areas—mechanical, administrative, general or electronics—you prefer.

After 36 months you can change your skill to another one if your abilities show you can do it. The air force will retrain you in this new work. But three years seems like forever if you are unhappy. Be sure you are signing on for the right job before you write your name on the contract.

With the contract signed, two more steps are needed to make you an airman. Your photo is taken for identification purposes and you are sworn into the air force. The oath begins this way: "I solemnly swear that I will support and defend the Constitution of the United States against all enemies, foreign and domestic…" And ends, "So help me God."

Congratulations, you're in the air force!

Male and female recruits should be prepared to face a tough basic-training period after they join the air force.

CHAPTER FIVE

YOUR FIRST RIBBON

You are disappointed that you can't leave for basic training that same day. It is rare when a new enlistee does. You might even be in the Delayed Enlistment Program, spending some time in the reserves while waiting for an opening in your skill.

Finally you report for active duty at the MEPS. You must tell your recruiter if, since your first visit there, your weight has changed, you've been seriously ill, you've had an operation, you've been arrested, you've received a traffic ticket, you've married (or divorced), or you wish to add on any dependents. Also, give your recruiter anything that should be included in your enlistment papers.

Then you're off to basic training at Lackland AFB. The air force pays your plane fare, arranges for your bus ride from the airport to the base and delivers you to the Reception Center no matter what time of day or night you arrive.

27

There you become one of about 45 new airmen assigned to form a **training flight** (as your group will be called). After eating a meal, you are introduced to your **military training instructor (TI)**. Then you march to your **dormitory**.

For the next six weeks, your instructor will be the most important person in your life. Whatever your instructor (man or woman) tells you to do, you do—and do it when you're told!

One sergeant remembers his arrival at Lackland. It was two in the morning when his training flight marched to their dormitory and were ordered to line up out front. Tired from the long day and the plane ride, they were almost asleep on their feet. Then they heard it: click, click, click. The new airmen, suddenly alert, had no idea what was happening. All but one remembered they had been ordered to keep their eyes looking straight ahead. The one who forgot turned his head just as the training instructor rounded the corner of the building. The TI blew up at him, ranting and raving in true sergeant form, teaching all the others that obeying orders is the best way to stay clear of trouble!

The clicking you hear comes from the metal taps a TI wears on the heels and sides of his shoes. He walks all day, and these protect his shoes from wearing out too soon.

There's another reason. The taps establish a rhythm when you march. In the beginning there are a series of thumps. Your shoes and those of the others don't hit the ground at the same time as the TI's shoes click. One day you hear one clicking sound; you and your TI are in sync!

That first night in your bunk you panic. Four (or six) years seems like a lifetime. You're homesick, even though you only left home that morning. It's a shock, realizing you know no one and are not sure what the future holds. Don't worry, it's a very normal reaction. Everyone at some time during basic feels that same way.

28

By the end of basic training, you'll probably find yourself in better
physical condition than you've ever been before.

Reveille sounds at 5:00 A.M. Breakfast is next (the time changes daily). From then until lights out at 9:00 P.M., you're busy every moment.

Basic can make or break you. If you keep the right attitude and you realize there's a reason for everything you do, you perform better and finish without any real problems. The TI isn't picking on you; he's trying to teach you how to work as a team.

All men and women receive the same training. The first few days are devoted to haircuts, collecting uniforms and equipment, getting immunization shots and settling in. Then the real training begins. It isn't easy. It's not meant to be.

You do the usual exercises—push-ups, sit-ups, running and stretching. You climb and crawl and fall flat on the ground. You sweat, you pant, you want to collapse.

You also take courses totaling 46 hours of classroom instruction. These include hygiene, military law, code of conduct, and personal affairs. In this last course you learn about pay, leave, allowances and various agencies on the base that can help you with personal problems.

You learn that the air force is the youngest of the armed services. A Balloon Section, established by the Army Signal Corps in 1892, was the beginning. In 1947 it was taken away from the army and made an independent armed service equal to the army and navy within the Department of Defense.

You learn a great deal, including how to fire an M16 rifle. Air force basic is the only armed service basic training that does *not* include combat arms.

By the end of the first four weeks, you run faster than you ever have—say, a mile and a half in under 14 minutes. Then there's the **obstacle course**, called the confidence course. Among other tests, you climb a rope ladder, crawl through a barbed-wire tunnel and go over 55-gallon drums stacked in a pyramid.

If you entered under the AIEP, before finishing basic you learn what special job skill you are best qualified to do. Once that has been decided, you know what your job will be.

You receive a ribbon to pin above your shirt pocket. You participate in the Graduation Day ceremony. You realize that you and those 45 strangers are now a team. Together you have shared and survived a strenuous experience and now you are confident that each of you will do a good job for the air force.

You're ready for training in your special skill.

These students of the Air Force Academy in Colorado are working toward a bachelor of science degree while preparing for careers as officers in the air force.

CHAPTER SIX

STRIPES ON YOUR SLEEVE

Where will you go next? It all depends on which skill you are scheduled to learn.

If you go in for security and police work, you remain at Lackland. Medicine's your interest? Your technical training is at another Texas base, Sheppard AFB at Wichita Falls. You enjoy typing, filing and office work. You go to Keesler AFB at Biloxi, Mississippi.

You've always wanted to know what makes planes fly. It takes millions of items to keep the air force operating. Do they ever run out of parts? How do they keep track of all the pieces needed? You opt for supply. Lowry AFB near Denver, Colorado, is where you find out the answers to your questions.

Some training is given at schools of one of the other services. To become a free-fall parachutist, you attend the army school. Underwater training is taken—you've guessed it!—at a navy school. Army Special Forces teaches you how to use scuba equipment. These skills are used mainly in rescue operations.

Technical training is like attending a civilian **vocational** school except you may march to and from classes. You live "on campus" (the base), share a dormitory room and may discover some or all of your classes are scheduled from 4 P.M. until midnight.

How long your training lasts varies according to the skill you are learning. With some you're finished in a few months; others take as long as a year. With basic behind you, discipline lets up. You develop more of a teacher-student relationship than was possible with your TI.

Next you're on your way to your first assignment. You may be sent to an air force base anywhere in the world. Sometimes you're trained to fix one kind of jet engine. You go where planes using that type of engine are based. If you trained in some other support areas, such as accounting, fuels or public affairs you could be sent to any base in the country or out of it. All bases need support work done, everything from administrative to vehicle operators. Without support the planes could not be flown.

Each base is like a town with stores, a library, hospital, gym and swimming pool. There are hangars, sheds and machine shops needed for work done on the planes. You may live on the base, depending on the availability of housing. Enlisted personnel live in bachelor airmen's quarters (housing). Married personnel may be assigned to family housing. If there are no openings, you may have to live off the base, but you have the same privileges as if you lived on it.

Sometime during your career you may be stationed overseas. Bases there have the same recreational and housing facilities.

When you are a new recruit your rank is airman basic. You do not have any insignia on your uniform. From there you progress up the ranks: airman, airman first class, senior airman,

You might be surprised to find that your housing in the air force has all the comforts of home, and maybe even more!

staff sergeant, technical sergeant, master sergeant, senior master sergeant, chief master sergeant, and possibly to the top enlisted **noncommissioned officer**, chief master sergeant of the air force.

To advance from one rank to another, you have to be promoted. Promotion is based on how well you perform your duties, length of time since you joined the service, length of time in your current rank and your **commanding officer's** approval. The time periods differ with each rank.

With each increase in rank, you add to the stripes you sewed on your sleeve when you became an airman. Airman first class adds another set of stripes. A senior airman has three sets of stripes. Little by little, the patch gets bigger.

The size of the patch on your sleeve is not the only item to get bigger. Your pay increases with each higher rank. Your pay rate is known as E-1, E-2 and on up to E-9. These are the same for all the armed forces. If you are an airman first class, you receive the same pay as the army's private first class, the marine's lance corporal and the navy and Coast Guard's seaman.

You're ready to take up your duties.

As part of an air force wing, your group is joined with several other groups serving under the direction of one commander.

CHAPTER SEVEN

"WHERE DO I FIT IN?"

You start your first **tour of duty** (length of time of your assignment; when you are reassigned, you begin a new tour of duty). The tour lasts for two or more years.

You know the air force is a large organization, but how is it set up? Most importantly, you ask yourself, "Where do I fit in?"

At basic, you were a part of a training flight of approximately 45 enlistees. Ten flights in different stages of training form a **squadron**. You are now a member of a squadron, which is the main building block of the air force.

With few exceptions, the whole air force is composed of squadrons. Yours and several other squadrons make up a **group**.

Your group joins other groups to form a **wing**.

Your wing is part of a numbered air force division of the United States (examples: First Air Force, Fifteenth Air Force).

Numbered air forces (NAF) are part of **major air commands**.

Air commands are the largest individual sections and together they form the United States Air Force.

Airmen trained in some nonflying skills, such as public affairs, find their squadrons assigned to a unit. A unit has many jobs and its squadrons cover many activities. It sounds complicated, but once you're in the service, it will sort itself out in your mind.

The air commands are like departments of a large corporation. From their names, you know what they do. In wartime the Air Combat Command (ACC) uses fighter aircraft and long-range bombers to knock out enemy installations or industries. Your recruiter is part of the **Air Training Command (ATC)**, which includes answering questions about the air force and the training of enlistees.

The **Air Mobility Command (AMC)** does just that—airlifts whatever needs to be flown from one location to another—including airplanes! Supplies are of first importance, but the AMC flies people too. *Air Force One,* the president's plane, is part of this command. In time of war soldiers are transported by AMC; in peacetime they are flown to new assignments. AMC has established regular air routes where the demand is heaviest.

But it's not all military missions. Bringing food to the Kurds was part of AMC; so was rescuing people from erupting Mount Saint Helens; throwing hay to freezing cattle was another; and so was airlifting food to Africa during one of the world's worst famines. Flying medicine, food and tents after a natural disaster has struck is all in the line of duty. The work of the AMC has saved thousands of lives.

To do this rescue work, you must volunteer and be specially trained.

(Photo right)   Airmen receive extensive training on fighter jets and bombers so that they will be prepared in the event of a war or sudden attack from an enemy.

Among other commands are the United States Air Forces in Europe (USAFE), Air Material Command (AMC), the Air University (AU), Space Command (AFSPACECOM) and Pacific Air Forces (PACAF). The Air Combat Command (ACC) must always be alert. Its members take to the air in fighter planes when an unidentified plane flies into our airspace.

Remember, you the airman are the most important ingredient. Regardless of your assignment, you are a vital participant in keeping the planes flying.

You've finished your technical training and you're not interested in more studying. Thought you were finished with textbooks, right?

You just might be wrong. Ninety-nine percent of airmen are high school graduates. The air force encourages you to continue your education. The fighting and flying elements of the air force are high tech. To do a better job, you must keep up with developments. The best way to do that is to use the air force programs to attend a qualified school.

Most programs are aimed at getting you interested in college-level courses. The air force pays most or all of your tuition and sometimes frees you from active duty to attend. If you are freed from active duty, the amount of time you spend in full-time college is added on to your active duty time.

There's the **Montgomery G.I. Bill**. Tell your recruiter if you wish to take advantage of this. You contribute $100 a month from your pay when you begin active duty. For the first year the money will be deducted. You cannot use those funds for two years; after two years of service you receive up to $350 a month for 36 months for a total of $12,600 toward your educational expenses.

But don't change your mind! Your $1,200 will *not* be refunded.

The Tuitions Assistance Program, the College Level Examination Program, the Community College of the Air Force and the Extension Course Institute are also available.

The last, ECI, is the most popular. It's the air force's correspondence school, which offers nearly 400 courses and is free. There must be something that appeals to you! How about apprentice carpentry?

Now's your chance to work toward becoming a college graduate—and an officer! One unusual feature of the Air Force Community College is that your technical training has been converted into college credits, which can be transferred to other educational institutions, and you receive four semester hours toward your physical education credits by the training you underwent at basic. Look into it!

Another way of becoming an officer is to attend the Air Force Academy near Colorado Springs, Colorado. This is a four-year course, offered to qualified students. The bluesuiter must apply directly to the academy.

Your dream of becoming a pilot and flying into the "wild blue yonder" just may come true!

If you should decide to join the air force, you will become a member of a proud team of people representing their country.

CHAPTER EIGHT

AS IT IS

Your life settles down to an eight-hour workday. You spend your free time as you wish. If you are stationed overseas, you spend leave sight-seeing and having your picture taken in front of Buckingham Palace or maybe a Roman fountain.

There are plenty of ways to amuse yourself without leaving the base. You are surprised to discover so many airmen involved in off-the-base community affairs. Some coach Little League, serve as Special Olympics volunteers, repair homes for the elderly and handicapped or visit local schools to tutor students.

Being an **active reservist** is a way of being a part-time airman. You must be 17 (with your parent's or guardian's consent until your 18th birthday) and under age 35 in order to join the Air Force Reserve. Enlistment must be six years *active* duty plus two years *inactive* for a total of eight years (the same as for a career airman).

You remain a civilian but undergo the same basic and technical school training that regular airmen take. You are on active status. After that you attend training assemblies with

The training and benefits you will receive from the air force will be of great value to you for many years to come. These reasons alone may persuade you to enlist. However, you should consider all the pros and cons before you make your final decision.

your reserve unit one weekend a month plus two weeks annual active duty. You can apply for the Reserve G.I. Bill.

Don't confuse *active* with *inactive* reserve. Inactive reservists do not have air force duties and they do not receive the same benefits as active-duty members. However, you can be called back into active duty. The inactive reserve is your assignment when you've finished your years as a regular and are awaiting the end of your enlistment contract.

The Air National Guard is another way of being a civilian involved with the air force. Requirements are almost the same as for the Air Force Reserve. While on active duty, you receive full military pay and privileges. In addition, you receive benefits from your state. These vary according to where you live.

Should you join the air force? Review all the reasons that appeal to you and all those that do not, and then make your decision. Don't rush into it. But whatever you decide, you now have the knowledge to reach an intelligent decision.

GLOSSARY

active reservist   A civilian who serves part-time in the air force but has a regular full-time job.

active service   As a member of the active service, the air force is your only job; you are a full-time airman with no other job.

air commands   Large individual sections of the air force. Similar to departments of a large corporation.

Air Mobility Command (AMC)   Flies whatever needs to be flown from one location to another (supplies, people, even aircraft).

Air Training Command (ATC)   In charge of training new recruits.

aircraft loadmaster   Person in charge of loading and unloading planes.

airman   Man or woman serving in the United States Air Force.

airman basic (E-1)   Your first rank and pay grade after you enlist in the air force.

Aptitude Index Enlistment Program (AIEP)   One of the programs under which a new recruit enlists in the air force.

Armed Services Vocational Aptitude Battery (ASVAB)   Test required of everyone who hopes to join one of the armed services.

avionics systems   Deals with flight control systems and radio and navigational equipment.

base   Government-owned property or property being used by one of the armed services.

basic training   Your first training after you report for duty. Through basic training, you learn to be an airman.

bluesuiter   An airman (man or woman).

bomber Type of aircraft that carries bombs and drops them on enemy territory.

commanding officer The person in charge. The command can be small, such as a training flight, or large, such as a wing.

Delayed Enlistment Program A program for enlisting under which you put off (delay) your reporting for active duty.

dormitory Building in which you sleep and keep your things.

Entrance National Agency Checks (ENTNAC) The agency that checks your background to be sure you are not a security risk to the United States.

E-1, E-2, E-3, up to E-9 Pay grades. Your pay grade sets the amount of money you receive. These grades are the same for all the armed services.

explosives ordnance disposal specialist Someone trained to dispose of dangerous explosives. Ordnance is the name for military supplies such as ammunition, bombs and fighting equipment.

group Several squadrons serving under one commander form a group.

Guaranteed Training Enlistment Program (GTEP) One type of program under which new recruits can enlist in the air force.

inactive reserve After you have finished your active service years, you are in the inactive reserve for the time remaining under your enlistment contract. You are also placed in the inactive reserve while in the Delayed Enlistment Program.

Junior Reserve Officers Training Corps (JROTC) A unit of active reservists just for high school students.

major air command Your wing and numbered air force are part of a major air command. The U.S. Air Force is made up of major air commands.

Military Entrance Processing Station (MEPS) At the MEPS you take your physical, pass a security check, decide the kind of work you hope to do in the air force, sign the enlistment contract and take the oath. You are "processed" from civilian to airman.

military training instructor (TI) The sergeant in charge of your instruction during basic training.

Montgomery G.I. Bill A congressional bill that provides a way for you to continue your education.

noncommissioned officer An enlisted airman from the rank of sergeant (E-4) on up. (Referred to as a noncom.)

obstacle course Objects (such as walls, barbed wire, tunnels) are placed in your path to block you from successfully completing the exercise. Also known as confidence course.

officer A person who has qualified for a commission, making that person higher in rank than enlisted personnel and noncommissioned officers.

recruit A person who has recently joined (enlisted in) one of the armed services.

recruiter A person who enlists new people in the armed services.

refueling plane Aircraft that carries a cargo of fuel to be transferred to another plane while both planes are in the air.

reveille A bugle call for the time to get up in the morning.

squadron Approximately 450 persons (ten flights of about 45 persons) form a squadron.

tour of duty Length of time of your assignment. When your tour is over, you are reassigned to the same place or transferred somewhere else.

training flight Approximately 45 new airmen form a training flight at basic training.

unit Some nonflying squadrons (such as public affairs) may be assigned to a unit.

vocational Refers to your work or profession. Also refers to training for a skill or work.

wing Several groups serving under one commander form a wing.

INDEX